Dolphins

Copyright 2020 - by Beth Costanzo

One of the cutest, smartest, and most playful ocean creatures is the **dolphin**. If you haven't seen a real-life **dolphin** in the wild or at your local aquarium, I'm sure that you have seen a picture of one in a book or on the Internet. The **dolphin** is a marine creature that is truly unforgettable.

www.adventuresofscubajack.com

While you may know some basic facts about the **dolphin**, there is plenty more to learn. To put it simply, the **dolphin** is one of the most fascinating creatures in our planet's waters. So come join me in taking a deep dive into everything you need to know about the **dolphin**. After learning these facts, you will be able to easily impress your family, friends, classmates, and teachers.

www.adventuresofscubajack.com

Some Fascinating Facts About Dolphins

www.adventuresofscubajack.com

In our study of **dolphins**, let's start with the thing that everyone immediately notices: its appearance. **Dolphins** are one of the largest sea creatures that we see. The average **dolphin** is about *5.5 feet* long and *110 pounds*. Having said this, some of the largest **dolphins** on our planet, like *the Maui's dolphin*, are about 31 feet long. *The killer whale, which is technically a **dolphin***, weighs about ten tons. To put it simply, you do not want to get in their path!

www.adventuresofscubajack.com

Besides their length and weight, **dolphins** have *torpedo-shaped* bodies. Their limbs over time modified into flippers and they have non-flexible necks. As you probably have already noticed, **dolphins** also have two fins: a large dorsal fin for stability and a tail fin to help propel itself through the ocean.

www.adventuresofscubajack.com

To breathe, **dolphins** release stale air from their blowhole and inhale fresh air into their lungs. You may even see this steamy spout from a **dolphin's blowhole** if you see a **dolphin** in the wild. Finally, **dolphins** have a layer of fat (called blubber) that helps keep them warm in cold water.

www.adventuresofscubajack.com

From the *dolphin's appearance*, let's now talk about where we can find **dolphins**. Beyond our local aquariums, **dolphins** can be found in oceans all around the world. For example, *the Burrunan dolphin* is found in *Southeast Australia*. *The Guiana dolphin* is found near *South America*. *The Atlantic spotted dolphin* and *Clymene dolphin* are found in the *Atlantic Ocean*. There are **dolphins** that are even found in the *Amazon River*! Ultimately, if you are near an ocean, there is a possibility that you will see a **dolphin** in the wild.

www.adventuresofscubajack.com

One of the most special things about the **dolphin** is that it has very well-developed *hearing*. This hearing is adapted for both air and water. In fact, dolphin's hearing is so excellent that some **dolphins** can survive even if they are blind. To communicate with each other, dolphins make high-frequency clicks that their ears can hear. The **dolphin** does have fairly good eyesight, but its ears are what separates it from other sea creatures.

www.adventuresofscubajack.com

Along with its sophisticated hearing, **dolphins** are extremely *smart*. To go one step further, **dolphins** are often thought of as one of the world's most intelligent animals. **Dolphins** have been known to act like humans in a variety of ways. For example, **dolphins** can teach, learn, cooperate, grieve, and scheme. This sort of intelligence is rarely found in other sea creatures or animals as a whole. Their brains are advanced and they rely on their brains to carry out all of these human-like functions.

www.adventuresofscubajack.com

At this point, you may be asking yourself: *"What about the jumping and leaping that dolphins do? Why do they do this?"* **Great questions!** One of the most noticeable things about **dolphins** is that they frequently *jump* above the water's surface. They do this for just a few seconds at a time, returning below the water to jump again. Ultimately, **dolphins** leap for a variety of reasons. If they are traveling, **dolphins** may choose to leap because it can save energy. But beyond that, **dolphins** may jump and leap to socialize, fight, communicate with each other in a non-verbal way, entertain each other, and even remove parasites from their bodies.

www.adventuresofscubajack.com

Now, let's talk about food. **Dolphins** feed on a wide variety of marine life. Some of their food includes fish, squid, seals, and other large mammals. Some larger **dolphin** species (like *killer whales*) even prey on smaller **dolphins**, but this is quite rare. When hunting a fish or large mammal, the dolphin uses its teeth to capture fast-moving prey. Because of its power and speed, **dolphins** can be extremely dangerous predators.

www.adventuresofscubajack.com

As far as predators of **dolphins**, there is good news. **Dolphins** don't have many marine enemies. Smaller species of **dolphins** have to watch out for sharks. That said, most of the danger comes from diseases and humans. In terms of diseases, dolphins can suffer from illnesses like a natural form of type 2 diabetes. This is a disease that humans also develop, so scientists are interested in further learning about the disease by studying **dolphins**.

Along with disease, humans pose one of the biggest threats to **dolphins**. Some humans hunt **dolphins** because dolphin meat is sometimes eaten (particularly in Japan and other Asian countries). Due to hunting and even environmental pollution, some **dolphin** species are even close to extinction. Those **dolphins** are mostly located in the *Amazon River*, but all **dolphins** are at risk of dying out from human activities.

www.adventuresofscubajack.com

More Fun Facts About Dolphins

As you can see, the dolphin is an extremely fascinating creature. If you want to learn more, here are eight fun facts about dolphins.

www.adventuresofscubajack.com

In Greek myths, dolphins were seen as helpers of humankind.

Dolphins are sometimes used to help humans deal with psychological problems and developmental diseases.

www.adventuresofscubajack.com

Dolphins have been trained for military purposes.

The earliest dolphins can be traced back to approximately 48 million years ago.

A group of dolphins is known as a "pod" or a "school."

While dolphins are generally calm with humans, several attacks have occurred, which have resulted in human injuries.

7

There have been some concerns about the human consumption of dolphin meat, as it contains high levels of mercury.

www.adventuresofscubajack.com

Dolphin Activities

www.adventuresofscubajack.com

Tracing

Trace the word then write it

Dolphin

Counting

Circle the correct answer

| 2 1 3 | 3 5 4 |
| 2 1 3 | 6 5 4 |

www.adventuresofscubajack.com

Maze

Help the Dolphin to reach the ball

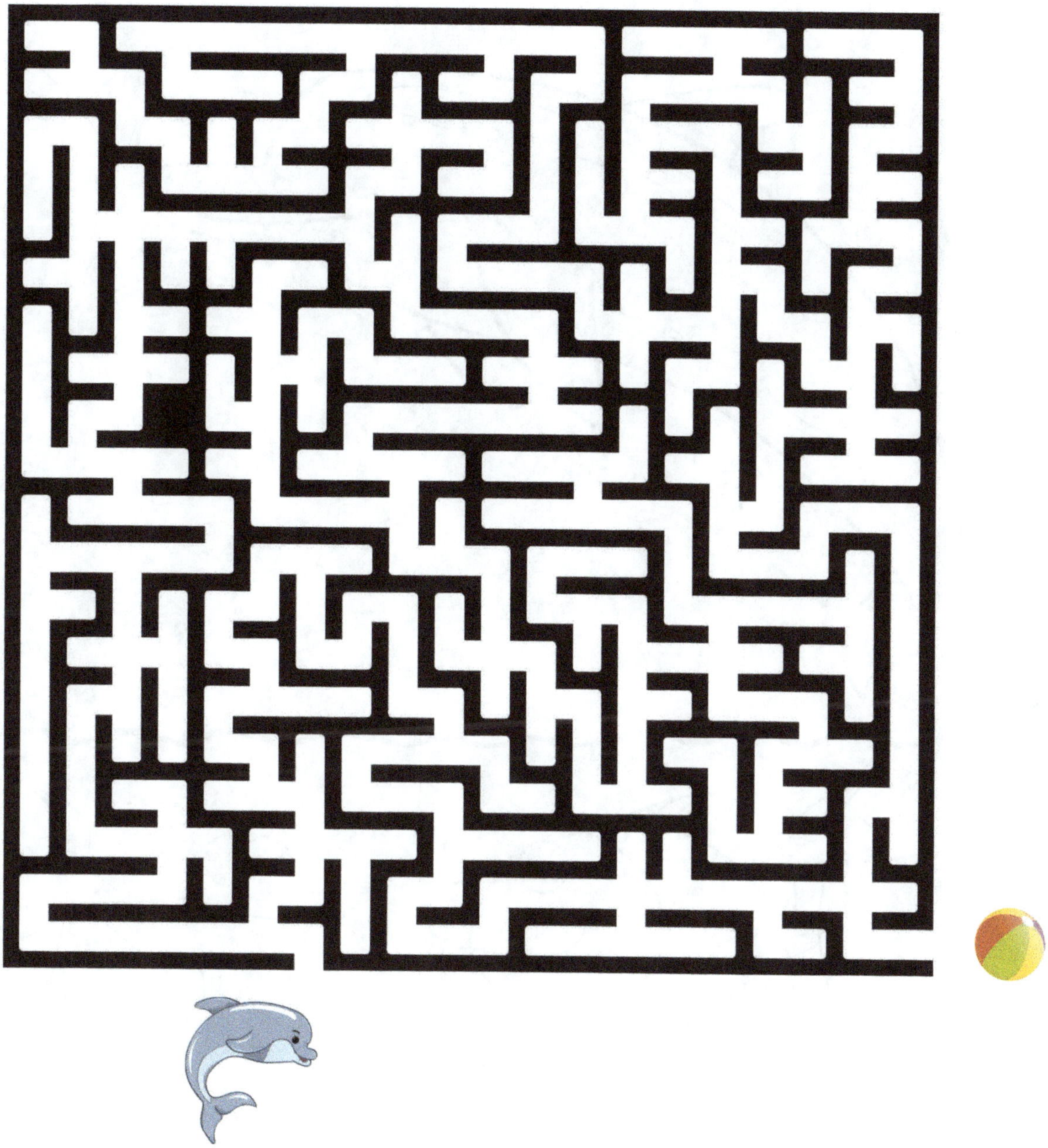

Coloring

Visit us at

www.adventuresofscubajack.com

And download this awesome Dolphin Activity Book, watch our amazing dolphin video and try your expertise with our super fun Dolphin Quiz.

www.ingramcontent.com/pod-product-compliance
Lightning Source LLC
Chambersburg PA
CBHW060429010526
44118CB00017B/2422